Protecting Resources

by June Lee

 **Harcourt**
SCHOOL PUBLISHERS

Orlando   Austin   New York   San Diego   Toronto   London

Visit *The Learning Site!*
www.harcourtschool.com

The Disappearing Soil

A strong gusty wind swept quickly across the plains in Oklahoma. Suddenly a huge, black cloud appeared. It looked like smoke coming out of a railroad train stack. Flora Robertson, on her farm, saw this cloud coming toward her. She didn't know what it was. She thought it was a storm, so she ran to the storm house. Outside, Mrs. Robertson's husband couldn't see anything in the darkness and had to use the fence to help guide him to the house.

Mrs. Robertson was frightened in the darkness. "We were all afraid . . . . We lit the lamp, and it was just so dark in there that we couldn't see one another, even with the lamp lit."

It was late afternoon, but the black cloud covered all of the sunlight. The darkness in the middle of the day was scary enough, but it was also a terrible struggle to breathe. "We just choked and smothered," Mrs. Robertson recalls.

A dust storm in the 1930s

A farm covered in dust

"We had to tie wet rags over our mouths just to keep from smothering." They soaked the rags over and over in a bucket of water. They continued this way while the black storm gusted fiercely for two hours.

When it was over, everyone was confused, and the house was covered with piles of fine dust. "The old-timers said they'd never seen anything like that, it seemed so fine. Our house was sealed, but that dust came through, somehow . . . . All around the doors and windows, dust would be piled so high," said Mrs. Robertson. "And you just had to mop real good when it was over to get it out. You just couldn't get it out any other way." Mrs. Robertson described these events about the dust storm of 1934 to researchers six years after the storm. That was when she and her family finally left the devastation in Oklahoma and moved to California. "You get afraid of staying there."

This unusual storm and many others like it were part of a difficult time in the history of the United States. What was happening? What was making the huge, black clouds? Why did the storms leave piles of fine dirt everywhere?

Geography played a role. These storms blew into an area of the country that included parts of Colorado, Kansas, New Mexico, Oklahoma, and Texas. This area is mostly flat and is part of the nation's Great Plains. Here, there are thousands of square miles of plains, some rolling hills, and few mountains.

Climate was also part of the problem. During the spring, strong winds are common in this area of the country. Gusty winds come rolling across the flat plains. Meanwhile, the area can have droughts, which are long, dry spells with no rain. The area was going through a period of drought at this time, so the soil on the farmlands was becoming drier and drier.

Farmers also contributed. For some time, the people of the nation had been eager to settle as much land as they could. The government helped people to farm the land. People wanted to work the acres of soil in the plains by growing crops. When there was no drought, wheat crops here did well.

A wheat crop in Kansas

At the start of the 1930s, the farmers were doing what they had always done to farm the land. They prepared the soil. They planted the seeds and watered the plants. When the plants grew, the farmers harvested them. Afterward, they cleared the leftover plants and turned over the soil to prepare for the next planting.

By the time of the drought, the soil on the farmland had become fine from the work the farmers had done on the land. Usually, soil contains dead plant material, making it lumpy, not grainy. After years of tilling, clearing, and turning, the soil had become like powder. New machines and blades cut the soil, turning it into fine-grained dust. Also, because there was little rain, not many plants grew to hold the soil down. Finally, the soil was left unplanted after crops failed because of the drought.

The soil had become fine and loose. There was nothing holding it down. As the strong winds came across the flat farmland, they picked up the loose soil. So much soil was picked up that it formed huge, black clouds.

The shape of the land, the windy climate, the period of drought, and the ways people farmed all helped make the dust storms in the plains. There were almost ten years of little rain and a lot of dust. Many acres of land were stripped of soil. As a result, this region became known as the Dust Bowl. Farmers could not successfully grow crops. Many lost their farms.

Taking Care of the Soil

The nation learned an important lesson from the Dust Bowl. We learned that if we did not take care of the land's soil, we would lose it.

To save the soil, the U.S. government started looking for better ways to work the land. The government worked with farmers to find ways to keep the soil from eroding, or wearing away. Almost 15 centimeters (5 in.) of topsoil was lost during the time of the dust storms. It takes an average of 500 years for just 2.5 centimeters (1 in.) of soil to build up!

To help save the soil and make richer soil today, farmers are practicing new ways of farming. One new method is called no-till farming. This method is sometimes called "ugly farming" because the cropland looks untidy to some people. People are used to seeing neat rows of soil and crops on farmland. No-till farming looks messy because farmers don't clear away the plant material left over after they harvest a crop. The farmers are not being lazy. They are actually working to make good soil. As the leftover plants die off, they give nutrients to the soil. The leftover plant material also makes a cover that protects the soil from blowing or washing away. The plant material also keeps water in the soil.

When it is time for new planting, the farmers plant their next crop through old plant material. The fields look messy because the old plant material shows between the rows of crops. The old plant material acts as mulch. Mulch is a material that is put on the ground to keep in moisture and keep out weeds. This conserves water and soil.

"Ugly farming" saves the soil.

Many farmers find that no-till farming makes the soil richer than it was before. One of these farmers is John Haas, who has a 1,600-hectare (4,000-acre) farm in southwestern Kansas. On almost all of it, he uses the no-till method.

"When the soil is left undisturbed it will start a renewal process. The structure or building blocks of the soil will improve," Mr. Haas told Congress in 2000. Congress was studying ways to improve the air, and it wanted to hear about how no-till farming could help.

Many farmers find it hard to change from their earlier ways of doing things. But more and more farmers are starting to try no-till methods.

"Great patience is . . . needed because when you have to deal with the large amounts of [old plant material], planting can be very difficult," said Mr. Haas. "Faith is another trait required . . . . to know what you are doing will really work when all your neighbors are still doing [what] your father and grandfather used to do."

In the past, wheat was the only crop farmers grew in these areas. There was, at one time, so much wheat produced here that this area became known as the nation's breadbasket. Today, you can see many different kinds of crops growing here. You can see fields of sunflowers, corn, and soybeans because the farmers are practicing crop rotation. Crop rotation is another method of saving the soil.

In crop rotation, a farmer grows one kind of plant in part of a field one year and a different kind of plant there the next year. By choosing plants that have different kinds of root shapes, the farmers can improve the condition of the soil. They can do this naturally, with plants, instead of with a plow. Also, by planting different plants, the farmer changes the kinds of nutrients in the soil. This is a way of rebuilding the soil to make it better for future plantings.

Sunflowers in Kansas

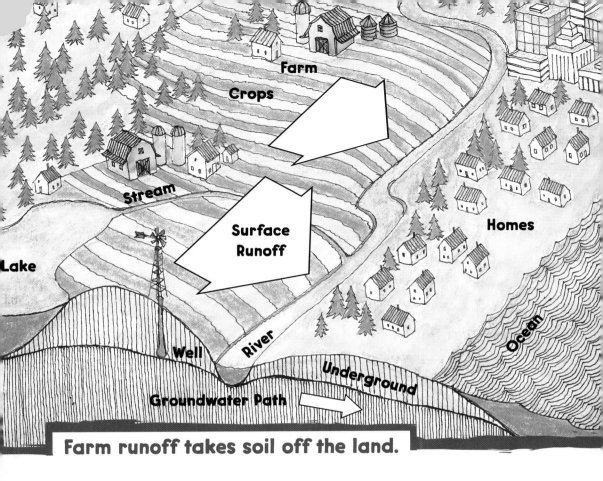

Farm **Crops** **Surface Runoff** **Stream** **Lake** **Homes** **Well** **River** **Underground** **Ocean** **Groundwater Path**

Farm runoff takes soil off the land.

Farmers and Runoff

Another way that farmers lose soil is through runoff. Runoff is water that washes off land and into nearby streams. Runoff is usually caused by rain. Water running off the land takes precious topsoil with it.

Runoff also takes chemicals with it. Farmers use chemicals to make the soil richer and to kill insects, weeds, and other pests. These chemicals wash off the land with runoff. Animals that live in the streams can be poisoned by the chemicals. The water from these streams may enter our drinking water systems and get into our bodies.

During the time of the dust storms, the U.S. government found new ways to stop soil erosion and keep water from running off farmland. The government asked farmers in Coon Valley, Wisconsin, to try its new ideas.

Engineers helped the farmers in Coon Valley switch to methods of farming that could help the land. They built terraces on the hillsides. Many people helped build these terraces. The terraces were made by flattening out slopes to keep the soil and water from running off easily. These terraces also gave the farmers more cropland.

The engineers also made contour strips. Instead of planting crops in rows up and down a slope, they planted them across a slope and in curves. This kept water from running straight down the hill.

Terraces flatten a hillside and make room for crops.

Contour strips keep water from flowing downhill.

"We didn't know what contour stripping was," Ernest Haugen told *Wisconsin Natural Resources* magazine in 2002. Mr. Haugen was just a young boy when his father had the engineers come to the farm, and he would follow the workers around the farm, curious to see how they shaped the land. "We did not know how to control soil erosion before 1934."

Farmers were also given tips for alternating strips of their main crop with strips of other kinds of plants. This is called strip cropping. The different kinds of plants slow down the runoff of nutrients and water.

Although the new ways of farming were strange to the farmers at first, they helped prevent runoff. Preventing runoff benefits both water and farmers—the water stays clean, and the farmers keep their soil. "Soil does not run away now," said Mr. Haugen's brother, Joseph Haugen. Engineers and geographers say that the erosion in Coon Valley has been reduced by at least 75 percent since 1934.

One farmer who benefits is Jack Ruger. Mr. Ruger has a 120-hectare (300-acre) farm in Indiana. He has planted a strip of trees, grass, and shrubs about 1.6 kilometer (1 mi) long on both sides of a creek that runs through his farm. The new plantings prevent runoff and help keep the water clean for the residents of Fort Wayne, where his creek water ends up.

The planting has also helped restore a wetland on Mr. Ruger's farm. A wetland is a marshy or swampy area where the soil is at least periodically covered by water. People used to think that wetlands were useless. They drained and filled wetlands to use for farmland. However, wetlands are very valuable. They act as sponges, absorbing water and keeping it from running off into streams. Wetlands also act as filters, cleaning chemicals out of the water in them.

"We need to restore some of the wetlands we've drained," Mr. Ruger told the National Resources Conservation Service, "although it's a problem because that's our most productive farm ground." Mr. Ruger knows that planting the new trees takes up land that would be good for farming. But he is willing to give up the land because that is the best way to conserve valuable resources.